Sensory Proc
Disorder

Parent's Guide To The Treatment Options You Need to Help Your
Child with SPD

Larry Jane Clew

ISBN: 978-1-63750-230-3

Table of Contents

Introduction

Sensory processing disorder is a disorder where the brain has trouble getting and giving an answer to information that comes in through the senses.

This is book explains Sensory Processing Disorder (SPD) in a simplified and precise way, and presents a drug-free approach that provides expect parents.

Over-responsivity--or under-responsivity--to touch or movement? A kid with SPD could be a "sensory avoider," withdrawing from touch, refusing to wear certain clothing, avoiding active games--or he might be considered a "sensory disregarder," needing a jump begin to obtain moving.

Over-responsivity--or under-responsivity--to sounds, sights taste, or smell? She may cover her ears or eyes, be considered a picky eater, or seem oblivious to sensory cues.

Cravings for sensation? The "sensory craver" never gets

enough of certain sensations, e.g., messy fun, spicy food, noisy action, and perpetual movement.

Poor sensory discrimination? She might not sense the difference between objects or experiences--unaware of what she's holding unless she looks and struggling to sense when she's falling or how exactly to catch herself.

Unusually high or low activity level? The kid could be constantly around the go--wearing out everyone around him--or move slowly and get tired easily, showing little desire for the world.

Some individuals with sensory processing disorder are oversensitive to things in their environment. Everyday noises or mind-boggling may hurt. The light touch of the t-shirt may chafe their skin.

Others with sensory processing disorder may:

- Be uncoordinated

- Bump into things

- Be hard to respond or react during play

Sensory processing problems are usually recognized in children. However, they can also affect adults. Sensory Processing Disorders are generally observed in developmental conditions like autism spectrum disorder. Sensory processing disorder is not just named a stand-alone disorder. Many experts believe that should change. This book offers simplified, clear information for parents and professionals--and a drug-free remedy approach for children.

Chapter 1

Understanding Sensory Processing Disorders

Sensory processing issues are problems with organizing and giving an answer to information that will come in through the senses. Kids with these issues may be oversensitive to sensory insight, under-sensitive, or both.

What exactly are sensory processing issues?

The word refers to troubles controlling information that will come in through the senses. These issues, sometimes called *Sensory Digesting Disorder* or *Sensory Integration Disorder*, can have a substantial effect on learning and everyday routine.

Sensory Processing Issues Truth Sheet

- Get yourself a one-page truth sheet on sensory digesting issues.

This overview can answer basic questions you might have about these complex issues. You'll find professional advice and insights, ways of use at home, and information on the best approach methods for your son or daughter at school.

If you believe your son or daughter may have sensory control issues, find out about actions you can take and ways to get help. And if you lately discovered your son or daughter has these problems, uncover what to do next.

What Sensory Control Issues are

In a few people, the mind has trouble organizing and giving an answer to information from the senses. Certain noises, places, smells, textures, and the likes can create a sense of *"sensory overload."* Shiny or flickering lamps, loud sounds, certain textures of food, and scratchy clothing are just some of the causes that can make kids feel overwhelmed and annoyed.

You will find two types of sensory processing challenges, and many kids experience a variety of the two. The first is **oversensitivity** (hypersensitivity). This leads to sensory avoiding-kids who avoid sensory insight because it's too overpowering. The other is *under-sensitivity* (hyposensitivity). This causes kids to be sensory seeking-they look to get more sensory stimulation.

- **Dyslexia Reality Sheet**

Readjust what a mother learned all about sensory issues from her child.

Often, kids with sensory digesting issues are oversensitive. They stay away from feelings they find intolerable.

However, many kids seek more sensory input, not less. They could want to touch things and feel physical contact and pressure. They could also be under-sensitive to pain and also have an unusually high tolerance for this. That's why they could prefer playing rough rather than understand if they're harming someone.

Some kids may be both sensory avoiding and sensory seeking. They might be oversensitive for some feelings and under-sensitive to others. A child's reactions can also differ from one day to another, or even during the day, concerning the environment or situation.

Sensory processing issues aren't a particular learning disability. However, they can have a significant effect on learning.

Sensory Processing Disorders Signs or symptoms

Everything you or your child's teacher might see depends upon two things. The foremost is the trigger-the sensory insight that's overwhelming your son or daughter. The second reason is the kind of sensory digesting challenge your son or daughter has.

Sensory Avoiding

Kids who are *sensory avoiding* may respond to an array of sets off. These range from loud sounds, unpleasant clothing, crowded areas, or certain food smells or textures, amongst others. Whatever the result is, the reaction can often be extreme.

Sensory overload can result in sensory meltdowns. These are extremely not the same as tantrums because they're from the child's control.

Below are a few other signs you may see in your son or daughter:

- Easily overwhelmed by people and places.

- Seeks out calm places in noisy, crowded conditions.

- Is easily startled by sudden sounds.

- Bothered by shiny light.

- Won't wear itchy or elsewhere uncomfortable clothing.

- Avoids coming in contact with people or hugging them.

- Includes a strong reaction to the consistency or smell of particular foods.

- Won't try new foods and has a minimal diet of preferred foods.

Gets upset about small changes in program or environment and avoids trying new things.

Sensory information isn't limited by the original five senses: sight, smell, taste, touch, and sound. *Interoception* is a lesser-known sense that can help you understand and feel what's happening within you. Kids who've trouble with interoception may have a harder time with toilet training or have a critical threshold for pain.

Two other senses, **body awareness** (*proprioception*) and **spatial orientation** (*the vestibular sense*), can also affect kids with sensory issues. Sensory avoidance of kids may cause trouble knowing where their personality lies with regards to other kids or their environment. Or they might be apprehensive about using playground equipment like the swings.

Sensory Seeking

Kids who are undersensitive to sensory insight have the

contrary situation. They often require movement. Plus, they may look for ideas like spicy or sour preferences and physical contact and pressure.

Below are a few other signs you may see in your son or daughter at different ages:

- Constantly touches objects

- Takes on roughly and calls for physical risks

- Includes a high tolerance for pain

- Often squirms and fidgets

- Is constantly on the road

- Invades other people's personal space

- Often gets distracted or feels anxious

- Is clumsy and uncoordinated

Note that kids aren't always one or the other. Some kids may be "sensory seeking" using situations and sensory "staying away" from in others, depending on how that child is coping or self-regulating at that time. That's why it's so important to see your child's reactions and also to make an effort to anticipate what causes them.

Other Conditions That Can Co-Occur with Sensory Processing Disorders

Sensory processing disorders aren't a diagnosis independently. However, they often co-occur with two conditions: *ADHD and Autism*. Kids don't need to have ADHD or autism to have sensory digesting issues. I had formed a meltdown, and, lastly, understood sensory overload.

Several indications of ADHD may look like the symptoms of sensory control issues. Kids with either of the conditions may need to maintain constant movement, for instance. However, the reasons would vary.

Like kids with ADHD, kids with sensory processing issues could also experience anxiety. Learn why kids with sensory issues could feel stressed.

Possible Factors behind Sensory Processing Disorders

Researchers want to know biological reasons for these issues. Some research suggests these issues can be hereditary. Experts are also looking at birth problems and other environmental factors. But up to now, there's no known reason behind sensory digesting issues.

ADHD and autism often co-occur with sensory issues. They don't cause them, however.

How Sensory Processing Disorders are Diagnosed

Sensory processing dysfunction aren't a formal diagnosis, although they used to be diagnosed as "sensory processing disorder." You may hear a specialist evaluator say something similar to, "Your son or daughter has trouble processing sensory information."

- **Steps to make Slime:** 3 Sensory-Friendly Recipes

There are many tests professionals may use to recognize sensory processing issues. Included in these are the Sensory Integration and Praxis Assessments (SIPA) and the Sensory Control Measure (SPM) checklist.

Generally, though, the behaviors kids show is evident

and palpable. It's essential to see your son or daughter and take down notes to talk about with experts who might identify your child's issues. Occupational therapists (OTs) tend to be qualified to recognize and create treatment plans for sensory challenges in kids. Other specialists might be able to identify sensory digesting issues, too. Included in these are:

- Pediatricians

- Developmental-behavioral pediatricians

- Psychologists, including neuropsychologists

School Evaluators

Monitoring your child's behavior and reaction will help you identify patterns and activates. Nonetheless, it can be hard to learn the place to start. Download a stress log to help determine why this is so when your son or daughter gets stressed.

How Professionals might help With Sensory Processing Disorders

You can find no medications for sensory processing issues. But some experts will help your son or daughter learn ways of dealing with sensory difficulties.

OT often uses kids with sensory issues. They help kids find ways to be less overwhelmed by sensory insight. You might have heard of a cure known as *Sensory Integration Therapy,* but more regularly, therapists might create what's called a *sensory diet.*

That is a tailored plan of activities. It can help kids figure out how to feel relaxed themselves and control their behavior and feelings. This makes them more available for learning and socializing.

Below are a few things that could be contained in a sensory diet:

- Jumping jacks

- Rolling on the therapy ball

- Push-ups

- Hopping along

- Climbing ladders and heading down slides

A few of these activities are heavy work, a kind of activity that pushes or pulls against your body. Read how heavy work can help kids with sensory digesting issues.

Child psychologists also use kids who've sensory control issues. They can use Cognitive Behavioral Therapy to help kids chat through their emotions and frustrations triggered by their problems.

At school, your son or daughter could probably get accommodations through a 504 plan. (If your son or daughter comes with an IEP for another concern, it might include accommodations for sensory issues, too.) The instructor could also give your son or daughter informal supports.

Classroom accommodations to help kids with sensory processing issues might include:

- Allowing your son or daughter to employ a fidget.

- Providing a calm space or earplugs for sound sensitivity.

- Telling your son or daughter in advance as regards to a change in routine.

- Seating your son or daughter from doors, windows, or humming lights.

- Allowing your son or daughter to consider exercise breaks to self-regulate.

See more accommodations for sensory digesting issues. See how to demand 504 arrange for your son or daughter. And get methods for speaking with your child's instructor about sensory issues.

Ways to Help Your Son Or Daughter With Sensory Control Issues

Coping with the unpredicted behaviors that include sensory issues can be hard overall, family. But knowing what's leading to them, it gets simpler to learn how to help. There are several strategies you may use at home and on the run:

- Learn how to produce a sensory travel package and get techniques for staying away from travel meltdowns.

- Explore sensory-friendly indoor activities.

- Uncover what to do if your son or daughter won't wear winter clothing.

- Download a six-week vacation planner for kids with sensory issues.

- Learn ways to help your grade-schooler offer with school issues.

Read developing a basis of self-advocacy in small children, as well as how to help grade-schoolers, middle-schoolers, and high-schoolers figure out how to self-advocate. Get tips about how to be an advocate for your son or daughter at school.

Chapter 2

15 Various Kinds of Sensory Issues Kids Cope with

1. SENSORY OVER-RESPONSIVE

Children who have a problem with sensory over-responsive disorder feel things intensely. They may be more likely to be excessively delicate when their senses are activated than the ordinary individual. A kid suffering from this kind of sensory disorder may feel timid from touch, noisy sounds, bright lamps, or intense tastes.

These children may experience "sensory defensiveness" when overly activated in virtually any of these ways. Sensory defensiveness is a "battle or airline flight" reaction, leading to a racing center, panicked sense, sweating, shaking, and adrenaline hurries.

The ultimate way to help children experiencing sensory over-responsive disorder is to avoid situations where he'll be overly stimulated. He might excel in an exclusive or charter college where course sizes are smaller, and he will not be subjected to overcrowded hallways or excessively loud classrooms. With therapy, children experiencing this disorder can figure out how to control situations where their senses are overly stimulated and continue to live completely healthy lives.

2. SENSORY UNDER-RESPONSIVE

Children who have problems with the sensory under-responsive disorder may go through the exact reverse of those working with sensory over-responsive disorder. They often show up withdrawn and self-absorbed or have emerged as silent and passive.

Children with this disorder don't feel sensory stimuli as much because of so many people. Because of this, a kid with sensory under-responsive disorder might not respond to summer or winter or usually react to pain. She gets slashes, scrapes, bumps, and bruises without realizing or sensing any pain, as she doesn't feel the tactile activation as a standard individual would.

Children experiencing sensory under-responsive disorder can be clumsy, bumping into things, and dropping down a great deal. This can be because it's problematic for these children to perceive the world around them credited to weak body consciousness.

3. SENSORY CRAVING

Children with sensory craving disorder crave excitement and seek it out actively every time they can. A kid with sensory craving disorder might not understand personal space and could always desire physical connection with other individuals. He might run into wall space, leap around, or wish to be continually coming in contact with and sense everything around him.

Most likely, the most frustrating thing concerning this kind of sensory disorder is that the stimulation doesn't calm the kid, but instead causes him to crave stimulation even more. Children with sensory craving disorder tend to be identified as having Attention Deficit Hyperactivity Disorder (ADHD) or Attention Deficit Disorder (ADD).

A child who's always moving, seeking, crashing, bumping, and touching may be Experiencing Sensory Craving Disorder. Some psychologists hesitate to diagnose a kid with sensory craving disorder individually from ADHD or ADD, while some feel a kid may be identified as having sensory craving disorder with no either of these conditions. The medical community is breaking up, and more research and observation is required to determine whether a kid can be identified as having Sensory Craving Disorder, lacking any ADD or ADHD analysis, or whether sensory craving disorder is an indicator associated with these disorders.

4. POSTURAL DISORDER

Children with the postural disorder may look lazy but could struggle with standing up and sitting down straight consequently as a result of insufficient control of eye motion and inner motion. Symptoms of postural disorder can include always slouching and leaning on furniture, wall space, or other folks whenever you can, reluctance to take part in sports activities, inadequate muscle firmness, reduced amounts, and fatigue.

A kid with this disorder could become isolated as he avoids taking part in activities with others in which moving is included. Children with this disorder may often sit down out of video games or activities for concern with falling, looking ridiculous, or not having the ability to keep up. They could also fall behind in college as they battle to sit upright in course, making them worn out and struggling to focus.

Postural disorder can be treated. Children with this sensory disorder should be motivated to stay energetic. As time passes, they can build primary and muscle power and overcome their insufficient balance and coordination. Therapy is also helpful in getting children who have a problem with postural disorder the assistance they have to thrive.

5. DYSPRAXIA

Children with dyspraxia battle to process sensory information correctly. Because of this, a kid with dyspraxia may have trouble learning new engine skills, planning things that want a series of occasions, and establishing goals.

A kid with dyspraxia may be accident susceptible and clumsy. She'll most likely have a problem with carrying out tasks that want excellent electric motor skills. She could also break playthings and have trouble with sports activities, especially the ones that involve tossing or getting a ball. She may try to face mask the disorder by refusing to take part in activities she understands she will have a problem with. She could also engage in dream play as this can be an area she feels safe and absolve to learn and grow and never have to take part in activities where she understands she'll have trouble.

Once more, therapy can be quite useful for children with dyspraxia. Like everything in life, practice makes perfect, and although children with dyspraxia may need to work harder to have success in activities that come simpler to other children, the higher the focus on mastering an art, the simpler the skill can be to allow them to perform.

6. AUDITORY

A child experiencing Auditory Processing Disorder, also called *Central Auditory Processing Disorder,* struggles with interpreting things he or she hears. He might battle to determine minor variations in the modulation of voice or individual sounds when there are undoubtedly several things happening. A kid with this disorder may hear just fine, and prosper when in a silent room without interruptions, but have hard time digesting information or instructions when they receive within an environment with a great deal taking place.

Diagnosis is best in supporting children with this disorder. As time passes and with therapy, children with auditory disorder can understand how to listen to, and process information in a manner that is practical to them. If this disorder goes undiagnosed, a kid fighting sensory disorder may have a problem with conversation, vocabulary, reading, and writing and fall behind in virtually any or many of these areas.

It is believed that up to 5% of children have problems with Auditory Processing Disorder. If a kid has a hard time pursuing directions, is easily side-tracked by sudden noises or loud noises, or gets annoyed in noisy, chaotic environments, he might be experiencing auditory digesting disorder.

7. VISUAL

A kid with visual control disorder struggles to seem

sensible of information processed through the eye. She may confuse the characters b and d, have a hard time concentrating on simple puzzles, knock over beverages, or spill things at mealtimes and bump into items or people. She could also battle to process different distances or have the ability to regulate how close or what lengths from her an object is.

Dyslexia is often called a *Visual Processing Disorder* and vice versa. Once more, views differ on if the two disorders are the same or completely independent of one another.

Therapy can be a significant element in assisting a kid experiencing Visual Control Disorder to see success in college. The main feature is pinpointing the disorder early and getting child help while contacts remain being created in mind. The earlier this disorder is recognized, the easier it'll be for a kid to overcome it.

8. TACTILE DEFENSIVENESS

Caucasian young man buttoning his shirt

A kid with tactile defensiveness is a lot more delicate to

touch than most individuals. He might be bothered by simple things that lots of us could not even think about. Things that may upset a kid with tactile defensiveness include, but aren't limited by, textured materials, things that are believed to be "messy," things that vibrate, hugs and kisses, sock seams, tags on t-shirts, bedsheets, filthy hands or face, lawn or fine sand on bare feet, blowing wind, blowing on bare pores and skin and even the shoes on his foot.

A kid who doesn't enjoy using sand, color, play-doh, food, or glitter in support; uses the tips of his fingertips to activate in these textures. Most children like this may be experiencing tactile defensiveness. He might also scream and cry when he must get outfitted or placed on socks and shoes.

With therapy, and as time passes, this disorder can be managed and overcome. The first rung on the ladder often recognizes a child's challenges with tactile defensiveness. After this has been decided, there are a lot of things that you can do to help treat and fight the disorder.

9. VESTIBULAR

The vestibular system is not just one of the five senses we are aware of but is possibly one of the most crucial ones. The vestibular system is linked to the liquid in the internal ear and aids with balance, coordination, and clear eyesight.

A kid with vestibular processing disorder may have a problem with hypo or hyper vestibular control, meaning that she will come across as sluggish, hyperactive, impulsive, or clumsy. A kid who is coping with this disorder in the hyper form may crave any activity where the feet are exercised, such as swinging, slipping, monkey bars, and bicycle driving or climbing. A kid who is working with the hypo form may dread, dislike, or avoid these activities no matter what.

Those experiencing vestibular processing disorder get dizzy quickly, or not get dizzy whatsoever after extreme spinning, prefer activities where little to no movement is necessary or love the feeling of twirling, rocking or tilting. Once a kid is diagnosed, therapy has shown quite effective in the treatment of this disorder.

10. PROPRIOCEPTIVE

Proprioception is our knowledge of our anatomies in space. It is what helps us regulate how much pressure to use when pressing a door open or raising a container of laundry. Children with Proprioceptive Digesting Disorder have a problem with their position in space, finding out how to move and knowing how much push to exert in a particular situation.

Signs a kid may be fighting this disorder are kicking or jumping legs while sitting down and heavily stomping foot while walking, enjoying the sensation of pressure when wrapped in a good blanket or laying underneath much object, pushing too much when coloring or writing, taking part in too much roughly plays with siblings or friends and frequently spilling or dropping things.

A kid with this disorder can overcome several symptoms through treatment. The very best medicine for a kid with this disorder may be time allocated to a playground where the guy can practice spatial recognition. Another great treatment Dad and mom won't mind having a kid assist parents with home tasks such as laundry or mowing the yard where lifting, tugging, or pushing is necessary.

11.GUSTATORY

Gustatory Processing Disorder impacts a child's sense of flavor. A kid with this disorder is quite sensitive to flavor, or has trouble determining what's and isn't appropriate to place into her mouth area.

Signs a kid has this disorder can include being truly a very picky eater, preferring food scorching or cold, constantly chewing things, and getting things in her mouth area (such as pens, playthings, or t-shirt sleeves), excessive drooling or a robust gag reflex. A kid with this disorder may love cleaning her tooth, the flavor of toothpaste and the dentist, or hate many of these things. She gets extremely stressed when asked to try new foods, especially people that have strong tastes or textures.

The very best ways to help children coping with gustatory processing disorder are: providing crunchy or chewy snacks during the day, providing toys that want use of the mouth area like bubbles or kazoos, or giving children hard candies which have a robust sour or sweet flavor.

12.OLFACTORY

Children with olfactory control disorder have a problem with things related to their sense of smell. A kid with this disorder may show some or all the pursuing symptoms: a desire to smell soaps, gas or other aromas with a solid fragrance, an aversion to feel which most people don't even notice, refusal to try particular foods predicated on smell, deciding whether they like someone centered on how the individual feels and a dislike of strong scents in perfumes and colognes or lotions.

A kid with this disorder may be helped in many ways. Help children recognize that smells are an integral part of the world around them. Acknowledge different scents each day and discuss what they are from and if a child loves them.

Once this disorder is identified, a kid who knows he's being heard when complaining about aversions to smell may significantly take advantage of the truth that others know very well what he is going right through. As mentioned, the ultimate way to fight sensory disorders in virtually any form is to recognize them and start treatment as soon as possible.

13.INTEROCEPTION

A kid who struggles with interoceptive processing has a hard time regulating physical systems such as sleeping, eliminating waste, eating, taking in, and even deep breathing. She may hate the sensation of food cravings, and taste often to remove the feeling or go directly to the bathroom frequently to avoid the feeling of having to visit. She could also love the emotions of craving for food and having to reduce herself, and even crave it, leading to her never to eat when she should and resist the desire when she must go directly to the bathroom. These activities can subsequently lead to bladder contamination or malnutrition.

The same holds as it pertains to sleep. Children with this disorder may rest a significant amount of or much too little. They could take deep breaths because they love the sensation of the environment relocating and out of their lungs, or make an effort to keep their breathing because the feeling is unpleasant to them.

Whatever way this disorder manifests itself, it's hard to deal with. Each one of these functions is essential for day-to-day life, and a kid who struggles to modify these activities could become quickly exasperating to parents. Show patience and seek help. This disorder is another that is highly treatable. Using the right support, any child can conquer it.

14.A COMBINED MIX OF THEM

Every case of sensory disorder differs. This makes the problem difficult to diagnose, treat, and understand, but headway has been made every day, and many children with sensory disorders are flourishing despite their frustrations.

Symptoms of the disorders are varied, and the severe natures of some conditions are incredibly significant, while some are relatively mild. A kid may have a problem with up to 8 different sensory concerns at one time, and could also have issues with varying subtypes within the eight primary categories.

Occupational therapists and psychologists who treat children experiencing sensory disorders are specialists in diagnosing each case in a manner that is patterned to the kid they may be treating. Just like each child is exclusive, each instance of a kid fighting sensory disorders is one-of-a-kind. Children with a specific treatment solution have nothing at all to fear.

15.AUTISM SPECTRUM DISORDER

Autism is more frequent in males than in ladies. 1 in 42 kids experiences some form of autism, while only one from every 189 women has the disorder.

The autism spectrum covers a variety, from moderate to severe. Many children who are identified as having autism also have a problem with sensory disorders. Some psychologists and doctors feel that a kid with a sensory disorder has autism, while some believe they aren't the same.

In any case, any child struggling to seem sensible of the world around him deserves love, support, and patience. This pretty new selection of disorders can be devastating for children. Fortunately, research has been conducted, treatments are being developed, and every day, we find out more and more what sensory disorders are and exactly how to take care of them.

If a child you understand is experiencing a sensory disorder, seek help. The earlier treatment is begun, the better chance a kid who is battling will have of leading a wholesome, happy life.

5 Methods to Support Students with Sensory Processing Disorders

Sensory processing disorder is seen as difficulties in accurately processing a variety of sensory information, such as touch, sound, and smell. It could be difficult for parents and educators to manage because of the two reverse ways it can express - *hypersensitivity* and *hyposensitivity.*

In over ten years employed in peadiatrics, I've seen how instructors with a much better knowledge of these children's needs have an incredible impact on the grade of a classroom. Therefore, it's essential to recognize which of the classifications your college student falls under before you think about how exactly to provide support.

Hypersensitivity

This is the child who actively avoids sensory stimulation. It's the kid who screams as though in pain at the audio of the hands' dryers in the toilet. Some of the phrases they make include:

- "Get it off me!" Children may be extremely private to the sensation of clothes, such as seams or brands. They might insist upon putting on clothing inside out to avoid the sensation of sure stitching or always want a specific T-shirt, whatever the weather. Grooming routines may also be complicated, especially, when worried about nails or locks.

- "It hurts!" Children with hypersensitivity often complain that one every day seems or looks "injured." This may be the sound of the vacuum or the light of the table lamp.

- "Yuck!" Smells may also be unwelcoming to children. Foods that don't trouble others may cause these to gag, leading to a particular diet plan.

- "Don't touch me!" Children with hypersensitivity who choose to play only with you shouldn't be handled or hugged; this might feel unpleasant to them. The sound of group play may also be unwelcoming`, leading to them to carefully turn away from an organization. The busyness of group play can be over-stimulating to children with SPD.

Hyposensitivity

"Why Did That College student Fail?" - A Diagnostic Method of Teaching

From Inquiry to Technology: A Reading List For Progressive Teachers

15 Types of Student-Centered Teaching

This consists of the thrill-seeking child who can't ever quite getting enough stimulation. This is the child who will come in from the playground, amazed to see that he's sliced himself because he didn't feel it or react. Typical markers are:

"Grrrr!" Hypersensitive children often appear frustrated, biting, or scratching themselves to accomplish any sensory feedback.

"Whoops!" Showing up clumsy or unacquainted with the non-public space of others, children with hyposensitivity have a problem judging distance and power. This means they often bang into other folks, slam doorways more forcefully than they ought to, or have trouble just seating still. They appear to crave motion and activities to keep up comfortable degrees of stimulation.

"Quickly, quickly!" Children with this kind of SPD often eat faster than they need to and, therefore, are more vulnerable to choking. There is also difficulty transitioning in one activity to another.

It's essential to notice that many of the signs may also be indicative of other disorders. For instance, children with autism often prefer playing alone, and the distraction that is included with a few of these aversions may be triggered by Attention Deficit Hyperactivity Disorder. That is difficult for diagnoses, and instructor input can certainly help pinpoint the framework of the behaviors to other experts.

Steps to making Life easier for kids with Sensory Processing Disorder

Sensory Processing Disorder (formerly known as *Sensory Integration Dysfunction*) is a disorder where the brain has difficulty processing incoming channels of information. Kids - and adults - with this disorder are either over- or under-responsive to sensory stimuli, which will make it much more problematic for them to handle the needs of life.

Regrettably, getting help for SPD can be difficult because the medical community can't even concur that it is present in any way - there is no recognized diagnosis.

Nonetheless, it absolutely can be found, insists Dr. Leah Light, director of Brainchild Institute in Hollywood, Florida. "Ask any mother or father whose child rips their clothes off because they feel too itchy, keeps their hands over their ear because noises are mind-boggling or gags as soon as a toothbrush is positioned in their mouth area whether Sensory Digesting Disorder is available. You may hear a resounding yes!" she tells you she knows.

The world can be considered a scary place for kids who've typical reactions to their sensory environments. And it could be scary for parents too. Whenever a child with SPD has regular meltdowns and problems with daily jobs, it's hard to learn where to start. Nevertheless, you do have the energy to help your child. Take a breath - and assume control.

The first rung on the ladder toward helping your son or daughter overcome their challenges is to determine what your child's particular likes, dislikes, and triggers are.

Is your son or daughter a sensory avoider or a sensory seeker?

The difference between kids who are sensory seekers and

kids who are sensory avoiders is mere that sensory seekers' systems have an increased threshold before information can be perceived, says Light. This implies they want more insight to decipher the message they want to understand. Alternatively, sensory avoiders have lower sensory thresholds, meaning a little amount of transmission provokes a considerable reaction. As a result of this, they avoid arousal since it overwhelms them. "Both sensory seekers and sensory avoiders may react with hyperactive behaviors, but also for different reasons," explains Light. "The first is seeking more insight and operating toward the stimulus, as the other is seeking less insight and running from the stimulus."

Kids who are sensory avoiders, i.e., delicate to particular feelings, such as audio, light or smell, may be attracted to activities offering extreme pressure to your skin, level of resistance to the muscles and insight to the bones since it calms them down when these are overstimulated, says Light. Alternatively, sensory-seeking kids are usually extremely active. They often respond favourably to very extreme types of sensory activation to check out as many ways as you possibly can to leap, fall, crash, kick, draw, push, suspend, lift, etc.

It's essential to keep in mind that your child differs from almost every other child - and various, even, from virtually every other child with SPD. Some kids may be oversensitive to feelings; others may be sensory-seeking, as well as others fluctuating between the two. They'll like some activities and hate others; it's an activity of learning from your errors. Also, your child's patterns may change depending on where they go, what's happening, who they are with, etc.

Ultimately, an activity of elimination can help you identify why your son or daughter feels happy and safe, and you may then provide them with opportunities to implement those ideas. This may mean peace and quietness under a weighted blanket, a few moments a day on the mini-trampoline or special headphones to filter noise at research time. When you have some notion of what your son or daughter needs, you can adapt your day to day activities and home routines appropriately.

How to incorporate sensory insight into everyday living with your sensory seeker

- Test out a weighted blanket, weighted vest, or weighted toy.

- Let your son or daughter help you with home chores, both indoors and out: moving furniture, vacuuming, transporting the laundry container, and digging in the gardening.

- Play the "sandwich game" - your son or daughter is situated between two pillows, and also you apply different degrees of pressure to the "sandwich" to work through what your son or daughter likes best, asking them, "Harder or softer?" as you press.

- Offer chewy foods or foods that are sour or spicy to stimulate flavor.

- Give "embracing squeezes" (deep-pressure squeezes) up your child's legs and arms.

- Give your son or daughter a racquetball or other rubbery subject.

- Dress your son or daughter in tight-fitting, elasticated clothing.

- Play tug of battle with a vintage towel.

- Take your son or daughter to the park and let him climb a tree or move down a hill.

- If your son or daughter struggles with visits to the dentist or hairdresser, provide them with a deep head massage therapy beforehand or let them wear a weighted hat. When you're working errands, let your son or daughter wear a backpack weighted with their choice of books.

How to incorporate sensory insight into an everyday routine using your sensory avoider

- Let your son or daughter play with dried out rice or fine sand, encouraging them to press it and run it through their hands. Cover a few cash in the rice or fine sand and ask them to dig for buried treasure.

- Use containers to try out with drinking water, pouring, and splashing.

- Play soft, slow music and encourage your son or daughter to move with time to the defeat.

- During meal preparation, invite your son or daughter to combine the element; let them blend, move and flatten dough; tenderize meats with a mallet; and help you bring pots, pans, and substances.

- During shower time, gently scrub your son or daughter with a washcloth or shower brush, test out a variety of soaps and lotions, use shaving cream or shower foam to create and attract on the wall structure and sprinkle the powder on your child's body and rub it to their pores and skin.

- Snuggle and keep your son or daughter often. Try softly touching their locks, face, and hearing and stroking them with a variety of textures: feathers, cotton balls, and vibrating massagers.

- For sensory avoiders, Light recommends offering only one kind of stimulus at the same time in a relaxed, quiet setting.

- Plenty of kids with SPD need predictability, so be sure you tell them in the required time if you want to make changes with their regular program or run unscheduled chores.

- It's important to identify signs that your son or daughter is now overstimulated, says the Celebrity Institute for Sensory Control Disorder. Included in these are unexpected yawning, hiccupping or burping, changes in pores and skin, extreme overactivity, and too much foolish or unsafe behaviour. If you observe these things, stop the experience immediately and do what works to calm your son or daughter down, such as wrapping them in a blanket, keeping them and rocking them gradually, or providing them with a warm shower or shower.

6 Methods to Help Your Son or Daughter Deal with Sensory Processing Disorders

Sensory Control Disorder: Sensory Processing Disorder relates to the mind and senses. It occurs when the brain has a problem managing and understanding the insight of thoughts.

Relating to a description by WebMD, SPD, is thought as a condition where the brain has trouble getting and giving an answer to information that will come in through the senses.

How to help your son or daughter deal up with each disorder

You will find four types of Sensory Processing Disorders namely,

- Visible - related to vision (eye)

- Auditory - related to sound (ears)

- Olfactory - related to flavour/taste (ears/tongue)

- Tactile - related to the epidermis (touch)

Let's breakdown each kind and know how you can help your son or daughter cope.

Children with Visual Sensory Control Disorder have trouble with inputs related to eyesight. Here are some ways to help children with such difficulties:

- **Don't be strict with vision contact:** Children with Visual Sensory Processing Disorder will find it hard to keep attention connection with anybody who's speaking with them. Usually, do not drive them to check out on you when they may be speaking with you or vice versa. Forcing them to check on you may disturb their focus. Instead, tell them that it's okay not to take a look at you, simplify out the problem, and ask these to acknowledge the fact they are hearing. If you're displaying them something, then guide them to check out it.

- **Everything related to lighting and lightening:** Shiny lighting might be upsetting. Make sure that you are modifying lighting and light configurations accordingly. Buy different dim lights that aren't very gloomy but are calming to the eye. Sunshine may be annoying to some children, but sunglasses can be a perfect solution. Even at college, request their instructor to situate their desk in a remarkable and well-shaded place.

- **Decrease the clutter:** A variety of different colours may be stressful with their eye and also make it hard to allow them to focus. Use delicate colors in their room and keep everything organized to sleep comfortably.

NOISE

Children who have a problem with Sound Sensory Control Disorders related to sound levels could find it hard to listen to sounds. This makes it hard to let them deal with sounds - for example, sound from a drilling machine or the audio of an aircraft, etc.

Here are some ways to help children with such difficulties:

- **Inform them beforehand:** If you are taking your

son or daughter out, inform them about what they might be hearing and the way to handle themselves in those situations. A good car horn could trouble them, so prepare them well beforehand so that no audio would take them by shock.

- **Hushed tones to the save:** Keep earplugs, noise cancellation earphones, etc. readily available always. You might have to test different kinds of ear safety devices to discover which best suit your child's needs.

- **New experiences:** As soon as you step outdoors, your son or daughter is forced to hear all types of different noises, which might not be pleasant to them. When you wish to take your son or daughter out to a supermarket, or a consumer electronics showroom, it might be smart to call the store beforehand and ask with them during what times they have a minimal crowd. After that, you can take your son or daughter at that time.

OLFACTORY AND TASTE

Children with Sensory Processing Disorders associated with olfactory/flavour issues may have problems with individual preferences and smells. For instance, the aroma of plants or the flavor of dairy might trouble them.

Here are some ways to help children with such issues:

- **Keep an eye on food allergies:** Your son or daughter may be suffering from particular tastes, which may differ from time to time. Their routine has a primary impact on how they feel with what they eat. It is smart to keep an eye on every action and its immediate effect on their diet.

- **Interpret the relation between smell and flavour:** There is undoubtedly rarely an instance where flavour and aroma aren't related. Our tastebuds identify the character, and olfactory senses determine the substance of the taste. This is the primary reason smell takes on an essential role for children with flavor sensitivities.

- **A quick flavor:** Children with sensitivities cannot eat a similar thing every day. Presenting these to new preferences and tastes is essential. Place the dish before them, and help them become more comfortable with the original recipe, reveal elements to them, to allow them to identify the ones they already like.

TACTILE

Children with Sensory Control Disorders related to real issues always would want to avoid touch from anybody. Also, they are delicate to certain materials and tend to be overwhelmed and annoyed when there is undoubtedly physical contact.

Here are some ways to help children with such issues:

- **Take them shopping:** Permit them to choose the fabric they find preferred. Be sure you permit them to use bed linens of their choice as well. Necessarily, everything they touch should be appropriate and comfortable with their skin.

- **Physical touch:** Most children with tactile sensitivity do nothing like anyone combing their hair or coming in contact with them. Ready your child before deciding to groom them or want to consider them for a haircut.

- **Find various ways of showing love:** Like a parent, you might feel enticed to hug your tiny one tightly in your hands, but that's not generally possible with children with Tactile Sensitivities. This won't mean there is absolutely no other way that you should show love. You can do so by speaking, lightly taking them in your hands using their consent, and putting on the fabric they prefer to touch.

Chapter 3

Guidelines for parenting a kid with Sensory Processing Disorder

Your child's disorder is not a reflection of you or your parenting. Taking a look at things for how they are really and letting go of the "why" or "how" it just happened can get us to a natural, open place. The truth is that parents of typical children or visitors of your family will question your strategy. They're usually from the area of attempting to help, but haven't any frame of research or experience with sensory children. Adhere to your guns! Only guess what happens is most beneficial for your sensory child as well as your family.

Forget about guilt and anger. If you are in a location of blame, guilt, or anger, you are making your sensory child's experience about you, which eliminates your capacity to advocate them effectively.

Value the presence of knowledge. Enter a habit of sitting and writing down a set of all the beautiful things you have discovered and experienced because of this to be the parent of the sensory child.

In the beginning, parenting a sensory child is a counterintuitive process. Why my work when parenting most common kids usually won't work just as for sensory kids is because it requires more careful thought and planning for the day to day activities to mother or father a sensory child. When you can keep an eye on that one idea, you'll be able to change and adjust your programs to the daily situations that could be a challenge.

Celebrate your child's strengths. Have a good knowledge of your sensory child's advantages. Write out a summary of all your child's excellent characteristics. Sensory kids are special and among a few of the most successful adults in the world. You will come across many people who won't understand or appreciate what they bring to the table, make sure you do!

Parenting a sensory child is a marathon, not a contest. Parenting is a trip, and with a sensory child, the tour will have many twists. Concentrate on the long-term goals and then create the steps and a need to get there.

No sensory solution works forever. Regular amendments will be needed to support your growing and ever-changing sensory child. All kids develop and change, and these changes can become more exaggerated for sensory kids. When you realize how to utilize framework, routines, and visible aids, you'll be able to find answers to the changing scenery you will face as time passes with your sensory child.

Brace up when you do everything wrong. The result is that you can find out more about how exactly to support your sensory child when something goes all wrong. Embrace the lessons in the "incorrect" experiences.

Be guided by love and understanding. Our sensory kids want to feel safe, adored, and comprehended. They are excellent kids who've trouble independently learning the guidelines of life. They want and want times every day when these are within an environment that they understand, which facilitates their method of viewing the world. You can do this on their behalf at home.

Move it on. One of the better long-term presents we can provide sensory children is to instruct them of the various tools. If you start educating your sensory child, your sensory child will have many years of practice, learning from your errors, and types of real success. The target is because this to be always a life-style to them, so when they may be in senior high school and sense overwhelmed, they stop and say, "What's my intention to handle this or get this done?" This is the description of self-reliance (and successful parenting).

The 6 Phases of Parenting a kid with SPD

- **#1 - Denial**

At 24 months old - "Huh, This is the terrible twos," I considered to myself thinking why his older sibling never really had "tantrums" that lasted more than one hour. I called this term "denial," as well as perhaps there was a little denial by the end, but it was me devoid of a clue on how the behavior helps him. I am truthful.

- **#2 - Self-Doubt**

At three years old - I felt all eyes were on me. There was

a day we were at the supermarket, the whole of the extended family; I internalized every one of his meltdowns of my failures as a mother or father. Whether it was my sister, my mother, my hubby - his behavior was the result of me screwing up. #truth

- **#3 - Anger**

Somewhere within 3 and 4 years, I started to become increasingly angrier with my child with myself. I couldn't realize why he behaved in these extreme ways, and I had formed zero ideas on how to react to him adequately. I don't keep in mind many concerns this time because, well, everybody knows what anger will do to your brains, right? I keep in mind feeling helpless, resentful, and filled with shame.

- **#4 - Knowledge**

At once, I began to assemble a whole load of information from the blogosphere, therapies, books, friends, and online forums. This stage was about educating myself and creating a supportive community around these parenting challenges. I needed knowledge and communication techniques for my back again pocket.

Resource: Quiet the Chaos Framework

The 6 Levels OF PARENTING A KID WITH SPD

- **#5 - Acceptance**

Around five years of age, I experienced an approval I didn't anticipate. This is the "it is exactly what it is" stage. I possibly could either play the credit cards life handed me, or I could be miserable, unsatisfied, and closed in my romantic relationship with my partner, my kids, my prolonged family, and my friends. So, we would embrace his characteristics as presents. The issues he faces daily are difficult; however, the features that drive him to the behavior are why it is unique and exceptional. He's fiercely loyal, finely detailed oriented, structured, and has professional functioning skills from the charts. His capability to learn people's feelings is undeniable. These characteristics translate into a grownup having the ability to make thoughtful decisions, to have conviction, and also to advocate for himself.

- **#6 - Empowerment**

This stage is the fun one. After taking the situation in the last step, I experienced more confidence than ever before in parenting my child. Now, my goal is to teach him on the fact that his extreme characteristics that bring hurdles to his lifestyle will be the same characteristics that provide him success and joy in life. Without approval of these characteristics and celebration of the traits, there is certainly little potential for him to be a happy, well-adjusted adult. I'll find ways to embrace his extreme characteristics again and again.

Chapter 4

Symptoms of Sensory Processing Disorder

Sensory Processing Disorder may affect one sense, like hearing, touch, or taste. Or it could influence multiple senses. And people can be over- or under-responsive to the things they have problems with. Like many illnesses, the symptoms of sensory control disorder exist on the spectrum.

In a few children, for example, the sound of the leaf blower beyond your window could cause them to vomit or dive under the table. They could scream when handled. They could recoil from the textures of particular foods.

But others appear unresponsive to anything around them. They could fail to react to extreme warmth or chills or even pain.

Many children with sensory processing disorder begin as

fussy babies who become stressed as they get older. These kids often don't deal well with change. They could frequently toss tantrums or have meltdowns. Many children have symptoms like these every once in a while. But therapists look at an analysis of Sensory Digesting Disorder when the symptoms become severe enough to have an effect on normal working and disrupt everyday living.

Factors behind Sensory Processing Disorder

The exact reason for sensory processing problems is not identified. But a research of some selected twins showed that hypersensitivity to light and sound might have a substantial genetic component.

Other experiments show that children with sensory processing disorders have irregular brain activity when they may be simultaneously subjected to light and sound.

Still, other experiments show that children with sensory processing problems will continue steadily to respond highly to a stroke on the hand or a loud sound, while other children quickly get accustomed to the sensations.

Treatment for Sensory Processing Disorder

Many families with an affected child find that it's hard to get help. That's because sensory processing disorder is not an acknowledged medical diagnosis at the moment.

Despite the insufficient widely accepted diagnostic requirements, occupational therapists commonly see and treat children and adults with sensory digesting problems.

However, in general, it entails assisting children do better at activities they're generally bad at and helping them get accustomed to things they cannot tolerate.

Treatment for sensory processing problems is named *Sensory Integration*. The purpose of sensory integration is to engage a kid in a great, playful way so they might figure out how to respond appropriately and function more normally.

One kind of therapy is named the **Developmental, Person Difference, Relationship-based (DIR) model**. The treatment originated through Stanley Greenspan, MD, and Serena Wieder, Ph.D. A significant part of the therapy is the "*floor-time*" method. The technique involves multiple classes of play with the kid and mother or father. The play periods last about 20 minutes.

Through the sessions, parents are first asked to check out the child's lead, even if the playtime behavior isn't typical. These activities allow the mother or father to "*get into*" the child's world.

This is accompanied by another phase, where parents use the play sessions to produce challenges for the kid. The issues help pull the kid into what Greenspan phone calls a "*distributed*" world with the mother or father. And the difficulties create opportunities for the kid to understand essential skills in areas such as:

- Relating

- Communicating

- Thinking

The classes are tailored to the child's needs. For example, if the kid would under-react to touch and audio, the parent must be very dynamic through the second stage of the play classes. If the kid overreacts to touch and sound, the parent should be more calming.

Signs or symptoms of Sensory Processing Disorder

Ask parents of kids with learning and behavioral disorders if their children experience issues with sensory disorder, and most of them will answer with a resounding **"yes."** Although it is broadly accepted that a lot of children with Autism Spectrum Disorders have trouble processing sensory insight, the fact that children who aren't on the spectrum also experience these issues to differing degrees is currently being analyzed more carefully by the special need community. While all children can appear quirky or particular about their needs and wants, children with Sensory Processing Disorder (also known as *Sensory Integration Dysfunction*) will also be severely suffering from their sensory choices that it inhibits their everyday activities. Sensory issues are usually thought of as either *hypersensitivity* (over-responsiveness) or *hyposensitivity* (under-responsiveness) to sensory stimuli. Below are some typically common indicators of Sensory Processing Disorder.

Hypersensitivities to sensory insight can include:

- Extreme response to or concern with sudden, high-pitched, noisy, or metallic noises like flushing toilets, clanking silverware, or other sounds that appear inoffensive to others.

- May notice or be distracted by background sounds that others don't appear to hear.

- Fearful of surprise, touch avoids hugs and cuddling despite having familiar adults.

- Seems fearful of crowds or avoids standing up near others.

- Doesn't like a game of label and is overly fearful of swings and playground equipment.

- Extremely fearful of climbing or falling, even though there is absolutely no real danger, i.e., doesn't like his / her feet to be off the bottom.

- Has poor balance, may fall often.

Hypo-sensitivities to sensory insight can include:

- A continuous need to touch people or textures, even though it's inappropriate to take action.

- Doesn't understand personal space even though same-age peers are old enough to comprehend it.

- Clumsy and uncoordinated movements.

- Exceptionally high tolerance for or indifference to pain.

- Often harms other children and pets when playing, i.e., doesn't understand his strengths and weaknesses.

- Is quite fidgety and struggling to sit still, enjoys movement-based play like content spinning, jumping, etc.

- Appears to be a "thrill seeker" and can be dangerous sometimes.

Chapter 5

5 Things You Need to Find Out About Dating Someone with Sensory Processing Disorder

Imagine a globe without sights, noises, and touches, you have this very immediate impact on how you feel and how you relate with people. Picture yourself getting up, grabbing a set of scissors, and eliminating the tags in each of your clothes you've worn going back two yrs. Envision covering your ear each time an open fire engine passes. How will you deal with clothing tags massaging against your skin layer, creating an itching feeling that never halts or touches that produce your skin feel just like it is burning? Imagine dating anyone who has these sensory overload encounters known as Sensory Control Disorder (SPD). Let me offer some dating advice for individuals who are participating with such a particular, magical person.

1. Adapt your mindset

Understand that your lover, as if you, is a distinctive being and person who is different from every other person in the world. What to do after all? Remember, you may want to revise, go-to day venues, or how you touch your lover. These variations can be challenging for a few to grasp, while some notice as a chance to form a connected once-in-a-lifetime relationship.

2. Spidey sense!

Truthfully, humans have eight senses. They may be:

- Olfactory system (smell)

- Visual system (view)

- Tactile System (touch)

- Gustatory System (taste)

- Auditory System (audio)

- Proprioceptive system (body consciousness)

- The vestibular system (balance)

- Interceptive System (condition of organs)

Although everyone has eight senses, it's important to note that each adult with SPD encounters a sensation range. This implies their sense level might over-respond or under-respond in single or multiple senses. For instance, one might like a music concert because they have an increased threshold of audio, while another may need to fix a period limit so that they do not become confused. Others avoid this said occasion because the stimulus is just too big and intense. If you wish to include your lover in activities, it could be done through bargain. You could speak to the gym supervisor to see when it's less crowded so that they do not become overwhelmed with machine sounds and side discussions. (Yes, your lover can experience many of these elements and quickly become overstimulated!) I would recommend discussing beforehand, as well as study your partner's senses to learn where your likenesses, distinctions, and thresholds stand. Having this romantic exchange allows both parties to get along about what to anticipate while going to outings and facilitate more distributed, memorable experiences.

3. Embrace Sense Uncomfortable

Speaking from experience, I am confident one learns more in one wrong than many privileges. For example, for you to learn how a person with SPD prefers to be kept, both parties will likely try to adapt. Precisely what does this mean? Touch, especially repeated caress in the same place without variance, might feel to your lover as though their pores and skin is burning. I want to be clear: It generally does not imply that you or your lover is at all broken. The feeling of what seems right and what can be tolerated has not yet been discovered. The situation mentioned above provides a chance for both parties to connect on a romantic level and honestly explain what emotions each currently seems to have. Moreover, it permits relationship development. She might say, "I love what you are doing, but it could feel better if you'd vary how you handled me and the location, i.e., light, hard, kneading, etc. -- on my arm." Entirely, be unstable. I graciously remind you having said that situations would probably arise as many people are different; however, continuous and immediate communication can help you as well as your partner connect and become on a single page.

4. Love through the stomach

Your lover might use a particular dietary intended to help regulate their body. At least, you ought to be supportive rather than sabotage it by insisting on going to restaurants the individual cannot go. I would recommend you interact and become adventurous with the new food selection. Apart from displaying you genuinely look after your lover, you could experience a delicious new dish and may feel healthier by eating healthier and natural foods.

5. Think long-term

A regular check-in to gauge your partner's sensation level is vital because these sensations often fluctuate.

Remember that agreed-upon programs may need to be postponed or canceled depending on how they feel. Keep in mind; it is alright if your lover becomes overstimulated. Your skill, if this occurs is to provide them with space to allow them to regulate themselves, knowing that everyone controls oneself differently. "Experience is merely the name we give our errors," once published, Oscar Wilde. Keep this at heart. Gain experience. And revel in the presence of fantastic, excellent company.

Steps to make a Sensory Bottle

Does your son or daughter have sensory control issues, ADHD, or a tendency to get overexcited? If so, she may have trouble soothing down even though you try soothing strategies. If your son or daughter is overwhelmed by sensory input, a sensory container can help. It's an instrument that will help kids self-regulate. You may even hear it known as a *neural tube*. The best thing as regards a sensory bottle is that it's a peaceful object your son or daughter can concentrate on. She may also tremble at it to get some good proprioceptive insight. And there will vary types of sensory containers to capture her attention entirely.

Your supplies will change depending on which kind of bottle you decide to make, but here will be the basics that you'll require to begin with on the homemade sensory container:

- A clean, empty plastic material drinking water bottle with the label removed

- Superglue (or a hot glue gun)

- Warm water

- Glitter

- Food coloring

- A funnel

- Corn syrup

Steps to make a Themed Sensory Container with Glitters

This sparkly sensory bottle is simple to make. It offers some visual relaxations for your son or daughter when she shakes it or has it around in her hands. Plus, it could be customized to your child's passions to make it more desirable. For example, if your son or daughter loves the sea, you may use blue food color, blue glitter, and confetti shaped-like seafood.

- First, squeeze corn syrup into a clear water bottle. Use enough to fill up one-third of the container with the syrup. (Rather than corn syrup, you may use essential oils, like in the video above.) Add tepid to warm water until it's about three-quarters full. Next, put in a few drops of food coloring and sprinkle in a few glitters. Place the cover on a water container and shake to combine the ingredients.

- Once you're contented with how it looks, fill up the container to the very best with water. Place the lid back again on and secure it with superglue or hot glue.

Steps to make an Influx Sensory Bottle

- Fill a clear water container about one-third full of

drinking water. Put in a few drops of food color. After the food colouring has passed on throughout water, fill those other entire containers with baby essential oil or cooking essential oil.

- Secure the cover with superglue. Your son or daughter can place the container on its part to start to see the waves or tremble it to begin to see the oil and drinking water separate.

Steps to make a "Peekaboo" Sensory Container with Sand

- A "peekaboo" sensory bottle can offer visual and tactile insight. It could also help your son or daughter stay concentrated better.

- You may make this bottle with rice that is dyed with food coloring (do some searching online for a recipe) or with colored play sand.

- Put a funnel in the mouth area of a clear water container and fill it up about halfway with fine sand or rice. Add small playthings, like alphabet beads, LEGO blocks, or mini-erasers.

- Then, fill those other entire bottles with fine sand or rice, leaving about an inch of room at the very top and thus giving the material room to go around and get confusing. Shake the container and then secure the cover with superglue.

If your son or daughter is a sensory-seeker, she may reap the benefits of substantial work activity using the container. The weight from it can soothe her as she transforms it around, looking for specific characters or objects.